BAD NEWS.
HE'S ESCAPED.

HE USED SOME OF THE ALIEN MACHINERY FROM MY FORTRESS.
WE LOST THE TRAIL. SOME KIND OF GRAVITATIONAL DISTORTION.
SO WHAT DO YOU WANT TO DO?
WHAT DO YOU THINK?
MAKE THE MOST OF IT.

...BATTERY JUST WENT DEAD ON ME LIKE THAT. SAME AS THE RADIO...
OH MY GOSH, ETHAN.
LOOK AT

HONEY, WAIT!
WE DON'T KNOW WHAT THAT IS! IT COULD BE AN ALIEN SPACESHIP OR IT MIGHT GIVE US WEIRD POWERS...
OR SOMEBODY COULD BE HURT, ETHAN.
IT'S NOT ALL LIKE IN...
OH.
IS HE HUMAN?
HOW VERY CHARMING.
I'VE JUST REVERSED ACROSS THE MATTER/ ANTIMATTER MEMBRANE IN A HOMEMADE SHIP AND THIS IS MY RECEPTION?
MY DEAR COUNTRY COUSIN, YOU ARE HUMAN...

I AM LUTHOR.
NOW... WHERE CAN I FIND THE SUPER-PEOPLE AROUND HERE?

THE JUSTICE LEAGUE OF AMERICA
J'ONN J'ONNZ— MANHUNTER FROM MARS
SUPERMAN
ULTRAMAN

WONDER WOMAN
BATMAN
GREEN LANTERN
FLASH
AQUAMAN
SUPERWOMAN
OWLMAN
POWER RING
JOHNNY QUICK
THE CRIME SYNDICATE OF AMERIKA

SEPARATE THE TAIL SECTION AND THE WING.
GET THE PEOPLE AWAY FROM THE EXPLOSIONS.
TELEPATHIC LINK ENGAGED.
LOUD AND CLEAR, J'ONN.
EVERYONE KNOWS WHAT TO DO.
AND IF NOT, WE'LL SOON LEARN.
I'LL TAKE THE FRONT SECTION, IF J'ONN HANDLES THE BACK.
FLAMES ARE OUT, J'ONN.
YOU ARE GREEN TO GO.
...STRANGE...
I CAN DETECT NO... UNNH... NO BRAIN ACTIVITY WITHIN...

NNN
NO ONE'S CONSCIOUS HERE. THE WHOLE CABIN'S ROLLING AND DEPRESSURIZED!
I MAY NEED SOME HELP!
ONE MOMENT, WONDER WOMAN...
I'M ON MY WAY.

I GOT 'EM ALL! WE GOT 'EM, SUPERMAN!
SO WHERE D'YOU WANT US TO PUT 'EM?
THE FLASH IS GENERATING A CUSHION OF PRESSURIZED AIR BELOW US. LOWER THEM GENTLY.
I DON'T HEAR HEARTBEATS...
OKAY
LET'S GET
THESE
PEOPLE ON THE
GROUND AND
I'LL SLOW DOWN
A LITTLE.
UH... BAD NEWS.
THEY'RE ALL DEAD.
AND LISTEN, GUYS...
I JUST CHECKED EVERYBODY FOR I.D.
STARTERS: A DOLLAR BILL WITH THE FACE OF BENEDICT ARNOLD WHERE GEORGE WASHINGTON SHOULD BE.
ANYBODY ELSE HEARING THAT LITTLE "X-FILES" WHISTLE ON THIS ONE?
THE UNITED STATES OF AMERIKA
IN MAMMON WE TRUST
ONE
ONE DOLLA

IF WHAT FLASH IS SAYING IS TRUE...
ANOTHER DIMENSION, J'ONN? WHERE HAVE THESE PEOPLE COME FROM?
WE CAN ONLY SPECULATE AT THIS STAGE, SUPERMAN.
AQUAMAN?
RIGHT HERE ON THE ATLANTIC SEABOARD.
HOW COME THE ONE PIECE OF WRECKAGE YOU MISSED LANDED ON MY ROOF?
WHAT HAPPENED? WHAT DID WE DO WRONG?
THEY WERE ALREADY DEAD, KYLE. WHEN THEY ARRIVED HERE THEY WERE DEAD.
YEAH, BUT WHAT KILLED 'EM?
AND WHERE DID THEY ARRIVE FROM...
WE'LL SOON...
OH.
HOW CURIOUS.
THEIR HEARTS ARE ON THE RIGHT SIDE OF THEIR BODIES.

THE WRECKAGE IS SAFELY DISPOSED OF, BUT IT APPEARS WE HAVE A MYSTERY ON OUR HANDS, SUPERMAN.
ARE THERE ANY CLUES ON THE FLIGHT RECORDER?
KKRUMPP
I'M READING SOMETHING ABOUT... A CALL FOR HELP... AND...
WAIT A MINUTE.
LUTHOR?
THIS IS AQUAMAN.
I THINK YOU SHOULD SEE THIS.
WHATEVER IT IS, IT DOESN'T LOOK LIKE THE 8:30 LEXCORP GOTHAM TO ATLANTA FLIGHT.

MORNING, MISS TESCHMACHER.
I'D LIKE YOU TO CANCEL ALL OF THE APPOINTMENTS IN MY DIARY.
BUT TELL THE PRESIDENT I LOVE HIM VERY MUCH.
PALM AND RETINAL SCANS: IDENTIFICATION POSITIVE: LUTHOR, L.
...MR. LUTHOR...?
MY OFFICE IS OFF-LIMITS TO EVERYONE BUT ME TODAY.
I FEEL A BRAIN WAVE OR TWO COMING IN, AND I INTEND TO SURF.

GOOD MORNING, EINSTEIN.
VOICE IDENTIFICATION POSITIVE: LEX LUTHOR.
CONTINUE TO SEARCH FOR GRAVITATIONAL ANOMALIES.
KEEP TRYING TO HACK THE JLA WATCHTOWER COMPUTER.
MY COUNTERPART ALMOST ESCAPED THIS MORNING. RE-ENCRYPT THE LOCKS; WE NEED HIM IN THERE FOR ANOTHER 48 HOURS.
ALSO I NEED HARD COPY: EVERYTHING WE'VE GOT ON THE AIRCRAFT THAT REVERSED OVER THIS MORNING.
OH... AND DIVERT FUNDING FROM OUR ARMAMENTS DIVISION TO... LET'S MAKE IT "GREENPEACE" THIS TIME.
AND ALL OF OUR EMPLOYEES COULD DO WITH A RAISE 200%? THREE.

FINALLY...
OPEN A SECURE INTERNET CONNECTION.
THANK YOU, EINSTEIN.
...
AH.
OPEN THE WINDOW, LUTHOR.

COME IN.
I WAS EXPECTING YOU.
THEN I'M SURE YOU KNOW WHY WE'RE HERE...

OF COURSE I DO. WHICH IS MORE THAN YOU KNOW ABOUT ME.
THE AIRCRAFT HAD NOTHING TO DO WITH MY ARRIVAL, AT LEAST NOT DIRECTLY.
I TRIED TO HELP THEM.

YOU LOOK SO LIKE HIM... AND YET...
CAN YOU SEE THE UNUSUAL MODIFICATIONS AT EVERY EIGHTH ANGSTROM IN HIS DNA?
HE ALSO HAS SEVERAL SOPHISTICATED TELEPATHIC LOCKS PROTECTING HIS THOUGHTS AND--
I'M NOT A LAB RAT...

THE JUSTICE LEAGUE. GOD BELOW.
MY NAME IS ALEXANDER LUTHOR...

I KNOW WHAT YOUR NAME IS, LEX, AND I'M TIRED OF YOUR DECEPTIONS.
THREE HUNDRED PEOPLE ARE DEAD! WHAT HAVE YOU DONE THIS TIME, LUTHOR?!
ALEXANDER LUTHOR, SIR.
AND I AM FROM THE FAR SIDE OF THE MIRROR, SUPERMAN.
MY EARTH ORBITS ITS STAR IN A COUNTERCLOCKWISE DIRECTION. HERE IT'S SUMMER, THERE WINTER.
YOU KNOW THIS IS TRUE; YOU SAW THE BODIES.
I WAS BORN IN AN ANTIMATTER REFLECTION OF YOUR UNIVERSE. WHERE I LIVE, GOOD IS EVIL AND VICE VERSA.
LOOK AT MY HEART!
YOU SAW THE EVIDENCE FROM THE PLANE!
THAT STRENGTH...
WHO ARE YOU?
PERHAPS YOU SHOULD COME WITH US... MR. LUTHOR.
THANK YOU.
I WAS HOPING FOR AN INVITATION.
MISS TESCHMACHER?
I'VE DEPOSITED $80,000 DOLLARS INTO YOUR ACCOUNT.
TAKE A NICE VACATION SOMEWHERE WARM.

THE UNITED STATES
ONE DOLLAR

DAILY PLANET
IN MAMMON WE TRUST

BY THE TIME THEY REALIZE THE NOTES ARE FAKE, THE ECONOMY WILL BE IN RUINS *AGAIN*.
AND NO *LUTHOR* TO STRUGGLE AND FAIL AS HE ALWAYS DOES. I'M ALMOST *BORED*.

WHAT DO YOU WANT, BRAINIAC? ARE YOU HERE TO SPOIL MY DAY?
MASTER.
OUR ATTEMPTS TO FOLLOW THE NEGITRON TRAIL OF LUTHOR'S ENGINE EXHAUST USING THE ACCELERATOR IN YOUR ULTRA-LABORATORY HAVE BEEN PARTIALLY SUCCESSFUL.

THERE IS NO SUCH THING AS A PARTIAL SUCCESS...
WAIT.
..NOT REAL! IT'S CRAP! IT'S JUST MORE CRAP FROM THE SKY! FROM ULTRAMAN!
I CAN'T TAKE ANY MORE OF THIS! I CAN'T TAKE ANY MORE OF THEM LOOKING DOWN AT US AS THOUGH WE'RE--
VVT
THEY INSULT ME WITHIN EARSHOT, THEY KNOW WHAT TO EXPECT.
BIG BROTHER IS WATCHING YOU.
GO ON, BRAINIAC.

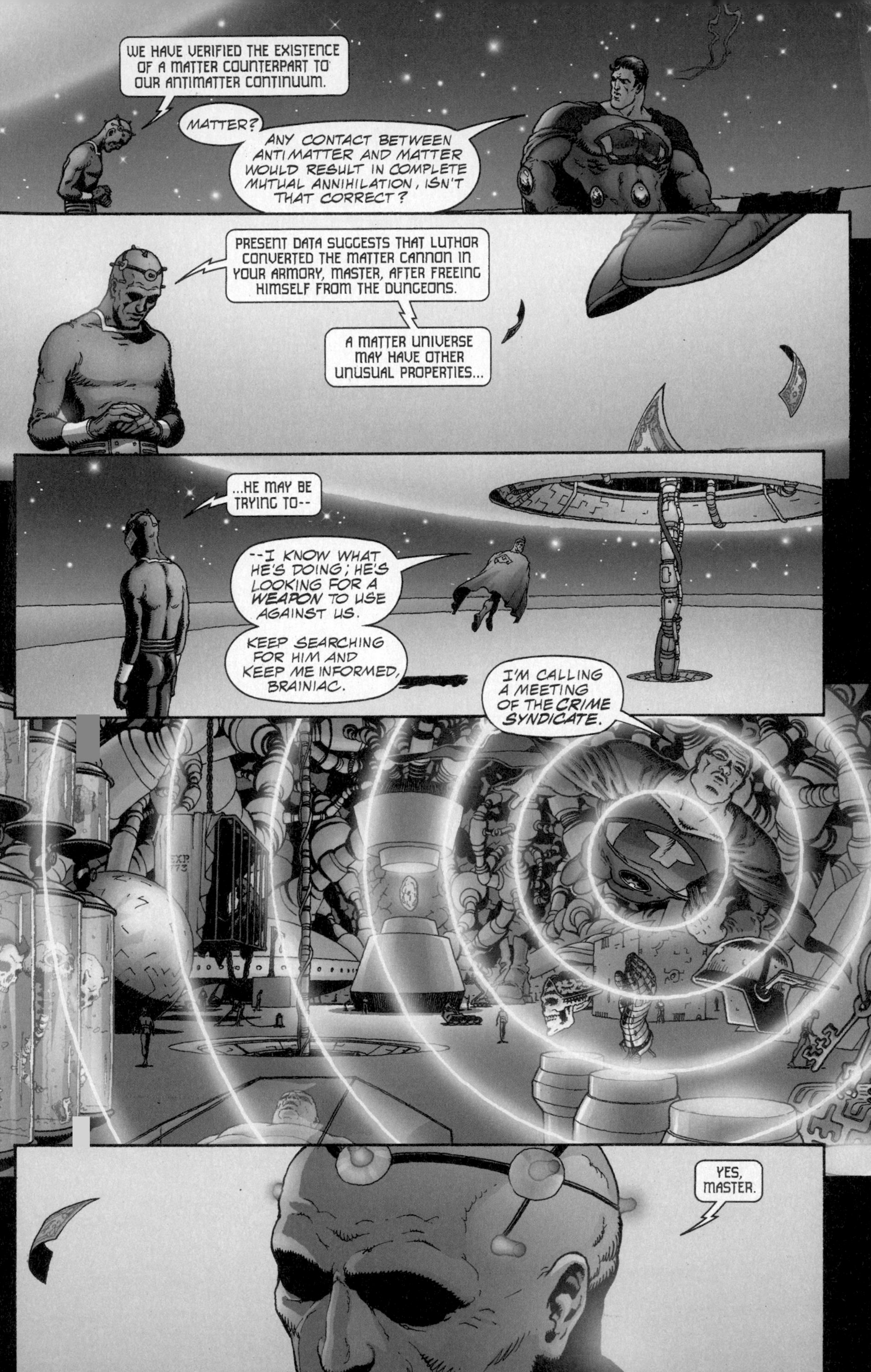
WE HAVE VERIFIED THE EXISTENCE OF A MATTER COUNTERPART TO OUR ANTIMATTER CONTINUUM.
MATTER?
ANY CONTACT BETWEEN ANTIMATTER AND MATTER WOULD RESULT IN COMPLETE MUTUAL ANNIHILATION, ISN'T THAT CORRECT?
PRESENT DATA SUGGESTS THAT LUTHOR CONVERTED THE MATTER CANNON IN YOUR ARMORY, MASTER, AFTER FREEING HIMSELF FROM THE DUNGEONS.
A MATTER UNIVERSE MAY HAVE OTHER UNUSUAL PROPERTIES...
...HE MAY BE TRYING TO--
--I KNOW WHAT HE'S DOING; HE'S LOOKING FOR A WEAPON TO USE AGAINST US.
KEEP SEARCHING FOR HIM AND KEEP ME INFORMED, BRAINIAC.
I'M CALLING A MEETING OF THE CRIME SYNDICATE.
YES, MASTER.

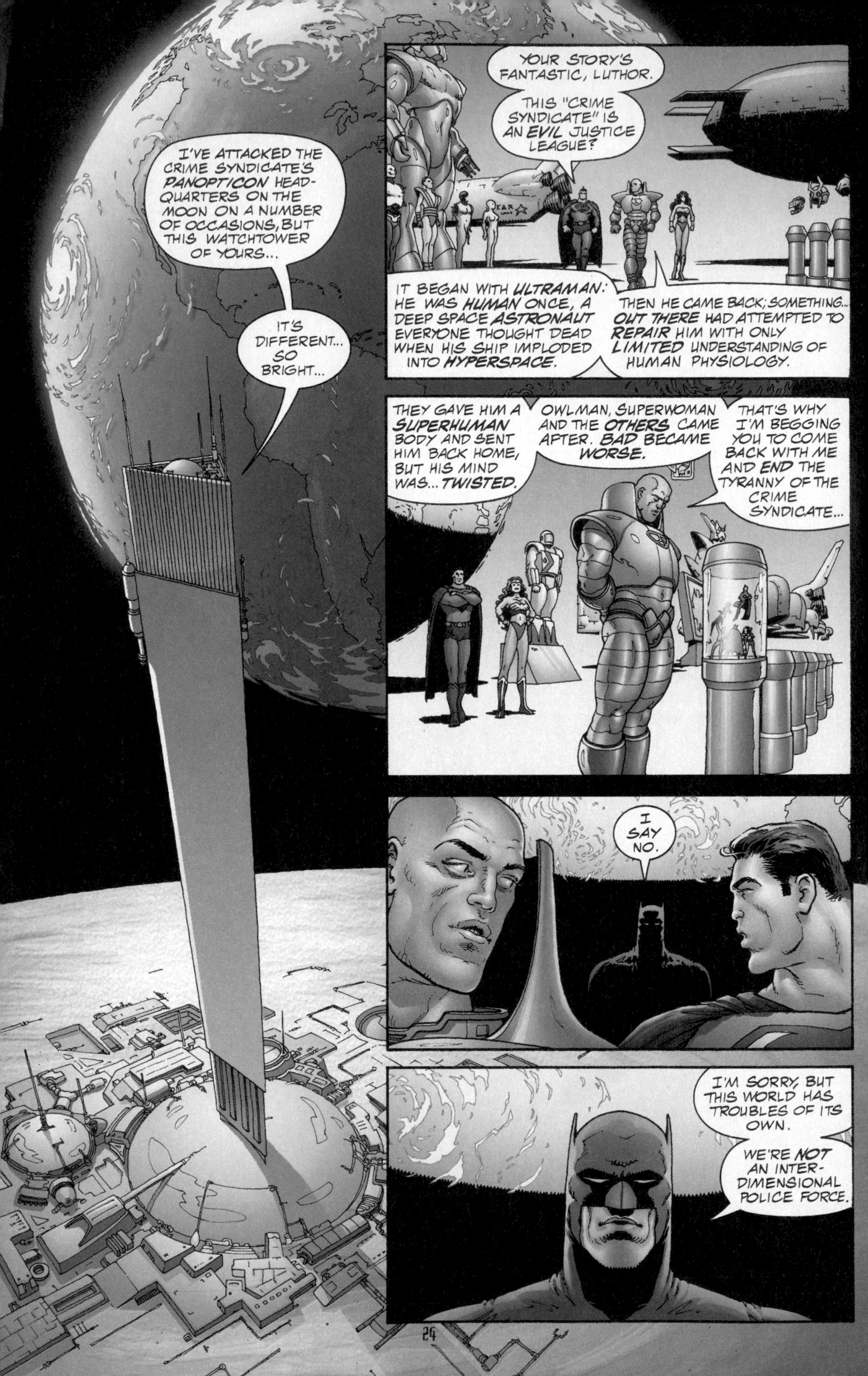
I'VE ATTACKED THE CRIME SYNDICATE'S PANOPTICON HEAD-QUARTERS ON THE MOON ON A NUMBER OF OCCASIONS, BUT THIS WATCHTOWER OF YOURS...
IT'S DIFFERENT... SO BRIGHT...
YOUR STORY'S FANTASTIC, LUTHOR.
THIS "CRIME SYNDICATE" IS AN EVIL JUSTICE LEAGUE?
IT BEGAN WITH ULTRAMAN: HE WAS HUMAN ONCE, A DEEP SPACE ASTRONAUT EVERYONE THOUGHT DEAD WHEN HIS SHIP IMPLODED INTO HYPERSPACE.
THEN HE CAME BACK; SOMETHING... OUT THERE HAD ATTEMPTED TO REPAIR HIM WITH ONLY LIMITED UNDERSTANDING OF HUMAN PHYSIOLOGY.
THEY GAVE HIM A SUPERHUMAN BODY AND SENT HIM BACK HOME, BUT HIS MIND WAS... TWISTED.
OWLMAN, SUPERWOMAN AND THE OTHERS CAME AFTER. BAD BECAME WORSE.
THAT'S WHY I'M BEGGING YOU TO COME BACK WITH ME AND END THE TYRANNY OF THE CRIME SYNDICATE...
I SAY NO.
I'M SORRY, BUT THIS WORLD HAS TROUBLES OF ITS OWN.
WE'RE NOT AN INTER-DIMENSIONAL POLICE FORCE.

WE CAN'T AFFORD TO BE: MY CITY NEEDS ME TO--
YOUR CITY? HOW DARE YOU!
LOOK AT YOU! SURROUNDED BY YOUR PEERS, SECURE IN YOUR SUCCESSES, ADMIRED BY A DOTING POPULATION.
DO YOU UNDERSTAND WHAT I'M TRYING TO TELL YOU?
ON MY WORLD, THERE'S ME! HEROISM IS A DIRTY WORD.
I RISKED EVERYTHING TO REACH THIS UNIVERSE. DON'T SEND ME BACK TO THAT HELL WITH JUST PLATITUDES!
HAVE YOU NO IDEA WHAT IT IS TO BE ALONE AGAINST A WORLD OF SHADOWS?
WHAT KIND OF HELP DO YOU NEED, LUTHOR?
FORTY-EIGHT HOURS. I WORKED IT OUT.
THAT'S ALL WE NEED TO CHANGE EVERYTHING.
WE CAN'T SPARE THE STAFF.
I SAY WE PUT IT TO A VOTE.

...IF WE TRULY STAND FOR JUSTICE, IF WE'RE GENUINELY COMMITTED TO SAVING LIVES AND PROTECTING THE INNOCENT FROM EVIL...
HOW CAN WE DENY LUTHOR?
HEY, I'M SOLD.
YEAH, I WANNA GO.
I MEAN EVERY SUPERHERO'S GOT TO MAKE AT LEAST ONE TRIP TO THE ANTIMATTER UNIVERSE, RIGHT?
I'M SORRY, SUPERMAN. WHILE I AGREE WITH YOU, I HAVE DUTIES AS THE MONARCH OF ATLANTIS...
ON THE OTHER HAND, YOU KNOW WHERE TO REACH ME IF THIS GETS OUT OF CONTROL.
I SEE NO ARGUMENT HERE.
LUTHOR IS A PROUD MAN AND YET HE'S RISKED HIS LIFE AND THE LIVES OF THE PEOPLE HE PROTECTS TO PLEAD FOR OUR AID.
YOU SAW HIS EYES, YOU SAW THE SCARS HE CARRIES.
ALONE AGAINST A WORLD OF EVIL, BATMAN.
I'VE MADE MY DECISION.
AQUAMAN STAYS. J'ONN STAYS.
I'LL TAKE THE VACATION.

WHEN I FOUND YOUR WORLD, I WASN'T SURE WHAT TO CALL IT-- "MATTER-EARTH," "ALTER-EARTH"...
IN THE END I KEPT IT SIMPLE.
I SETTLED ON EARTH 2.
STRAP YOURSELVES IN FOR THE REVERSAL.
THEY'RE GONE.
J'ONN... IF THERE ARE COMPLICATIONS...
THEN LET US PRAY YOU AND I ARE THE EQUAL OF THEM, ARTHUR.

I DON'T DEAL WITH BOSS GORDON AND I DON'T DEAL WITH THE OWLMAN.
I'M MEETING YOU HERE TO ARREST YOU AND PUT YOU ON TRIAL AND HAVE YOU EXECUTED.
WHATEVER YOU'VE GOT TO TRADE, WE DON'T NEED, OWLMAN.
AND WHERE YOU'RE GOING THERE'S NOTHING YOU'LL NEED EITHER!
SHOW YOURSELF! I KNOW YOU'RE...
...THERE...
BUT YOU DON'T KNOW WHERE, DO YOU, OLD MAN?
YOU SHOULD HAVE TRADED.
HE'S HERE! HIT THE...

LLLLUUHHHSS
OPEN FIRE!
OPEN FIRE!
AIRBAG.
WHOMP
STRIGIFORM HIRE
STRIGIFORM HIRE

STRIGIFORM HIRE
GCPD
I HAVE RAZORANGS AND BLOODSEEKERS. SMART GUYS RUN.
SMART GUYS OR DEAD GUYS?
YOU'RE NAILED, MOTHER...
ON THE CONTRARY.
OUCH.
STRIGIFORM HIRE
THE GOOD DIE YOUNG IN GOTHAM.
HEH.
YOU TOOK YOUR TIME.
SO WHAT WAS ALL THAT ABOUT?
THIRTY COPS SUPPORT WAYNE IN THE GCPD. SATAN KNOWS WHERE HE FINDS THEM BUT THEY'RE ALL HERE ON DISK, AND AS SOON AS WE'VE DEALT WITH ULTRAMAN'S CRIME SYNDICATE EMERGENCY...
I'M GOING TO FIND THEM TOO...

...NO, DON'T. ULTRAMAN WILL SEE...
MM
UURRMM.
MAYBE HE LIKES TO WATCH.
THE EMERGENCY SIGNAL'S STILL BUZZING...
...THE SIGNAL...
YEAH.
GUESS YOU'RE RIGHT.
LET'S GO.

...LUTHOR'S DISCOVERED A UNIVERSE COMPOSED OF MATTER INSTEAD OF ANTIMATTER.
DO WE PANIC?
OR DOES THE FACT THAT THE MOST PERSISTENT THREAT TO EVERYTHING WE REPRESENT JUST VANISHED FROM THIS UNIVERSE CALL FOR A CELEBRATION?
YOU TELL US, BOSS.
CSA
CUI BONO
WELL, LUTHOR BEING OUT OF TOWN'S GOOD FOR BUSINESS, RIGHT?
THEORETICALLY SUCH A MATTER UNIVERSE WOULD INCLUDE MATTER DUPLICATES OF ALL THE STARS AND PLANETS, INCLUDING EARTH.
I DIDN'T SAY THAT. IT'S THE RING.
IT'S A GOOD POINT.
ANOTHER WORLD TO CONQUER.

EXACTLY. EXACTLY WHAT I'M SAYING. ULTRAMAN'S TOTALLY RIGHT.
WE SHOULD BE THINKING ABOUT HOW WE CAN EXPLOIT THIS.
IF LUTHOR WANTS A CHALLENGE, HE'LL GET ONE. THINK OF THIS MATTER UNIVERSE AS JUST ONE MORE VULNERABLE FREIGHTER LADEN WITH TREASURE.
HOIST THE JOLLY ROGER HIGH...
AND PREPARE TO BOARD.
WHAT WAS THAT PIRATE DRIVEL?
TALK TO ME. WHAT DOES "MATTER DUPLICATES" OF OURSELVES IMPLY TO YOU? IT WAS YOUR TECHNOLOGY LUTHOR USED TO ESCAPE...
I'LL SPEAK TO YOU AFTER I SPEAK TO HER.
ONE OF THESE DAYS YOU'LL GO TOO FAR, OWLMAN, AND YOU WON'T COME BACK.
DOCTOR NOON
WHITE CAT
SURE.
UNTIL THEN I HAVE THE NEGATIVES, REMEMBER?
ONE DAY.

UHHH.
THAAAT RRRING, MAN... WHASS ALLL THAT ABOUT...
LOOSE! YOU WANNA SHOOT THAT JUICE, MAN?
THE SLO-MO'S DRIVING ME CRAZY. I'M TRYING TO TAKE A LEAK HERE AND YOU SOUND LIKE A DRAIN.
SSUHYOOO
WISH I'D NEVER SEEN THIS THING.
BASTARD TOLD ME IT WAS A CURSE BUT I WAS TOO DUMB TO CARE.
NOW I GOT SOME TIBETAN FREAK CALLED VOLTHOOM CRAWLING AROUND IN MY HEAD...
BUT HEY! I GOT THE POWER!
POWA RING
CHECK IT OUT, DUDE!
FF
YEAHHH LAAATER, YUH KNOOOO
MMMMCOMING UPONNNN
WWELLTHETHING ISTHIS: THE MORE YOU THINK ABOUT IT, THE MORE OBVIOUS IT GETS.
A MATTER UNIVERSE MEANS MATTER VERSIONS OF US.
COULD BE THE BEST FIGHT WE EVER HAD, MAN.

...WAIT.
YOU TALK TO ME!
HANDS OFF!
YOU SEE THIS?
ONE DAY I'LL HANG YOU WITH THIS.
BITCH.
SORRY TO INTERRUPT, ROMEO...
I'VE BEEN THINKING ABOUT THIS AND THERE'S SOMETHING YOU OUGHT TO KNOW...

GREAT KRYPTON... I'VE NEVER SEEN ANYTHING LIKE THIS PLACE, LUTHOR.
IT'S SO GRIM AND...
NOW SHOWING
THE THREE RACKETEERS
FORD

HEY!
LEAVE THE DOG ALONE!
NO...
24 HOURS

WHAT'S YOUR PROBLEM, DUDE?
DOG DIDN'T DO NOTHING TO YOU...
HEY, PRETTY BOY!
I'M GONNA SHUT YOUR WEIRDO...

...AH...
IT'S POWER RING!
CRIME SYNDICATE

I SAY WE ACT NOW WHILE WE STILL HAVE SURPRISE ON OUR SIDE.

REA

LOCAL
OUTTA HERE

THE ELEMENT OF SURPRISE IS ALL WE HAVE!
EASY, LUTHOR.
SOMEONE KICKED A DOG, YOUNG MAN, GET USED TO IT.
THERE ARE PEOPLE SUFFERING OUT THERE!

OKAY, OKAY... THIS IS NOT WHAT I'M USED TO, OKAY?
I DON'T LIKE THIS PLACE, MAN.
THEN HELP ME CHANGE IT!
WE NEED YOU TO SECURE THE PANOPTICON, NOT TO INVOLVE YOURSELF IN STREET BRAWLS!
IT'S HARD FOR US TO STAND BACK AND WATCH, LUTHOR...

GREEN LANTERN, THE MOON'S ALL YOURS.

...GUYS ARE SCARED, TOM. THESE MEN AND WOMEN HAVE FAMILIES.
THE BASTARD'S GOT NAMES AND ADDRESSES ON THAT DISK.
WE CAN STILL GET HIM.
TOM, YOU'RE ON YOUR OWN.
YOU SHOULD GO HOME. YOU DON'T LOOK SO GOOD.
COMMISSIONER WAYNE
WE CAN STILL STOP HIM...
COMMISSIONER WAYNE?
NEWS UPDATE IN FIVE

I... CAME TO TALK.
I...

I KNOW YOU BLAME ME FOR YOUR MOTHER'S DEATH THAT NIGHT. I KNOW YOU BLAME ME FOR BRUCE. THERE IS NOTHING LEFT TO TALK ABOUT, THOMAS!
I PROMISE... I'LL KILL YOU FOR WHAT YOU'VE DONE TO ME AND I WILL FEEL NO! MORE! GUILT!

YOU'D BE GUILTY OF MURDERING THE WRONG MAN, THAT'S ALL.
I'M NOT THOMAS. I'M NOT OWLMAN.

MY NAME IS... BATMAN.
I'M SORRY TO HEAR ABOUT YOUR FAMILY.

WHATEVER STUPID NAME YOU CALL YOURSELF...

I...I KNOW MY OWN SON... I...

HE'S CANTEEN JERKY, COMMISSIONER.

CHA-CHAKK

EVERYBODY HERE'S GOT A GRUDGE. YOU SAY THE WORD.

IN LESS THAN TWELVE HOURS THE CRIME SYNDICATE'S GLOBAL OPERATIONS WILL *CEASE*.

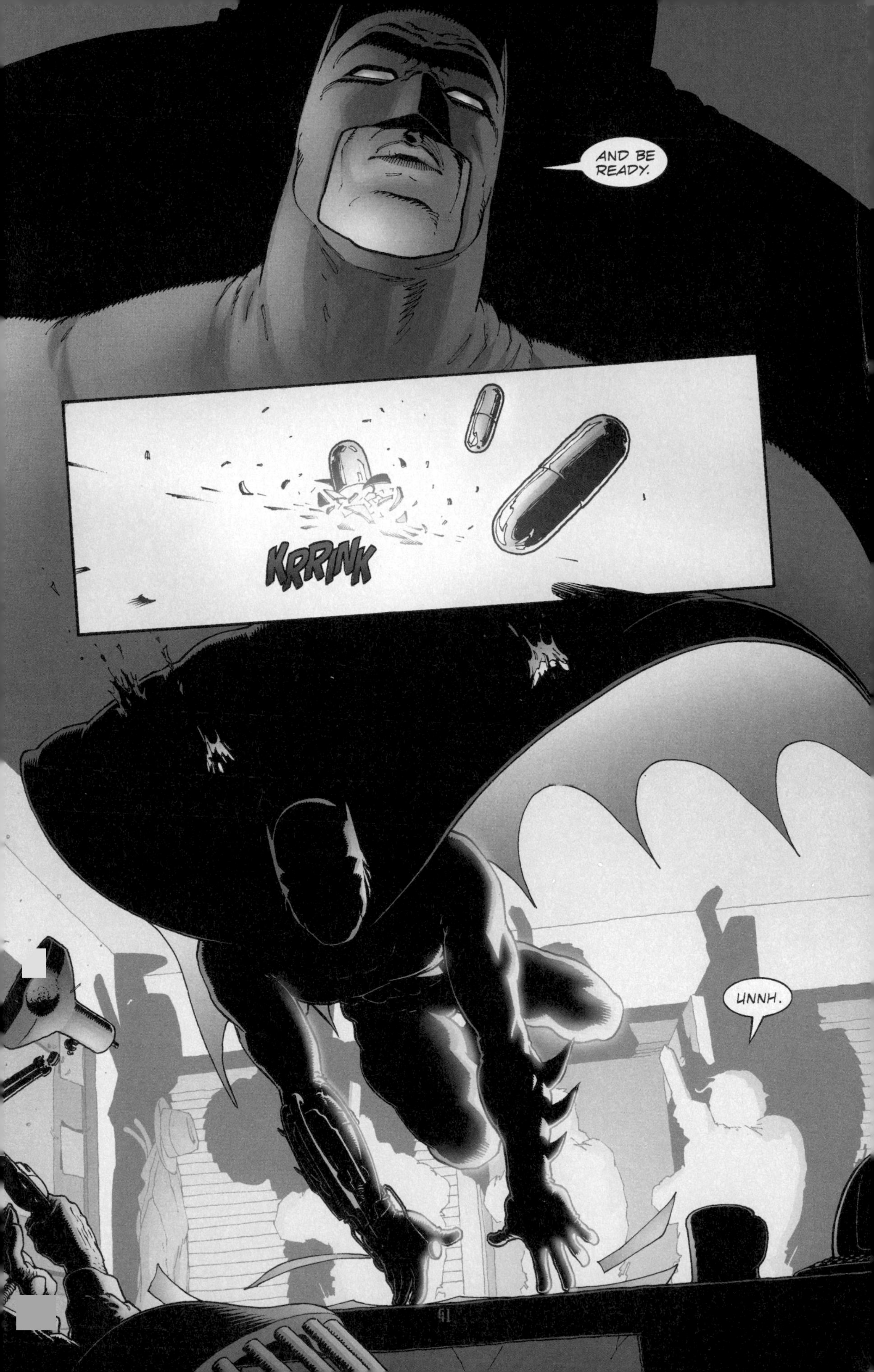
AND BE READY.
KRRINK
UNNH.

DAMN!
I'M SEEING FIREWORKS...
I CAN GET HIM!
NO! STOP!
DON'T SHOOT!
...DON'T SHOOT...

I HAVE... RESERVATIONS ABOUT THIS, DIANA.
IF THIS WORLD AND THE CRIME SYNDICATE ARE OUR OPPOSITES IN EVERY WAY...
ROYALIST TERRORISTS HANGED
HOW WILL WHAT WE DO HERE BE REFLECTED BACK HOME?
EVIL ISN'T THE REFLECTION OF GOOD, BATMAN. GOOD IS THE REFLECTION OF GOOD.
WE CAN POLISH THE MIRROR, THEN IT'S UP TO LUTHOR TO...
HERE'S SUPERMAN NOW.
THE BIG SMOKE
HIDE MONTHLY
THESE PEOPLE ARE LIVING IN A NIGHTMARE; I'VE NEVER SEEN SUCH MISERY AND HATRED.
GREEN LANTERN'S IN POSITION ON THE MOON AND ONLY ONE CRIME SYNDICATE MEMBER IS ABSENT FROM THEIR PANOPTICON.
THEN WE'RE ALMOST READY.
JOIN LUTHOR IN ULTRAMAN'S FORTRESS AND LEAVE SUPERWOMAN TO ME AND MY MUSTACHE.
I HOPE WE'RE ALL ABSOLUTELY SURE WE'RE DOING THE RIGHT THING...
WHATEVER THAT MEANS HERE.

TELLING YOU WE'RE TRAPPED.
IF THIS IS YOUR FAULT, ULTRAMAN'S GONNA KICK YOUR ASS PAST JUPITER!
WHAT? COME ON! I'VE BEEN TAKING A LEAK HERE!
THAT WAS FOREVER AGO! I'M TALKING ABOUT THIS!
SEE?
THAT'S NOT ME...
IT WASN'T ME.
AWARE OF A PLASMA PRISON OF UNIDENTIFIED ORIGIN.
WIPE THAT STUPID GRIN OFF YOUR STUPID FACE AND TELL ME WHAT IT IS YOU--
SHUT UP!
...LOOK...
IT'S GREEN.
EVERYTHING IS GREEN, MAN...

LY PLANET
NGO BIG $$$ BINGO BIG $$$ B
THE MOON'S *WHAT?* GET PICTURES AND *PROVE* IT, FAKE 'EM IF YOU HAVE TO...
I DON'T *CARE* IF IT'S NOT TRUE... I DON'T *CARE* IF IT'LL RUIN YOU.
RECEPTION
DAILY PLANET FREAKSHOW PLANECRASH HEARTS ON LEFT

RECEPTION
DAILY PLANET EUROSTATES TO BOMB EVIL BRITAIN NUKES FOR NOOKY
DAILY PLANET RIPPER PICS 8 PAGE 3-D INSERT
DAILY PLANET ELVIS EXECUTION PAY-FOR-VIEW RECORD
YOU'RE TOMORROW'S *FRONT PAGE,* SWEETHEART.
?

...UH...HI, *CAT*... I, UH...
I WONDERED IF *LOIS* WAS...
LIEUTENANT CLARK *KENT?* WHAT'S WITH THE *WIMP* ACT, SPACE RANGER?
MARRIAGE TO QUEEN BITCH TURNED YOU GAY?
CAN'T SAY I BLAME YOU.

ANY TIME YOU WANT TO ORBIT SOMETHING A LITTLE LESS *ARCTIC,* JUST WHISTLE.
I SURE WILL. LOIS IS?...
LOIS LANE EDITOR

SHE WENT TO POWDER HER NOSE WITH LITTLE *JENNY OLSEN* IN TOW.
IF YOU RUN YOU MIGHT CATCH HER SQUEEZING HIS *ZITS* FOR HIM...
UH... THANKS, CAT. I THINK I KNOW THE WAY.
FREAK.

STORE ROOM

STORE ROOM
YOU'RE THE ONLY ONE WHO KNOWS MY LITTLE SECRET, JIMMY...

LOIS LANE IS *SUPERWOMAN*. THE *ULTIMATE* FRONT PAGE HEADLINE...

THAT WOULD MAKE *ANY* CUB REPORTER'S CAREER, WOULDN'T IT?

BUT YOU EVER BREATHE A WORD AND I'LL SKIN YOU.
SLOWLY.
WITH MY FINGERNAILS.

YOU LIKE WATCHING ME CHANGE TO SUPERWOMAN, DON'T YOU, YOU LITTLE CREEP?
YOU MAKE ME SO SICK.

SUPERWOMAN'S SNITCH, JIMMY OLSEN.
THAT'S WHAT YOUR OWN NEWSPAPER CALLS YOU.
CUH... CUH... CAN I... CAN...

NO.
UURRF.

I SHOULD...
SNFF

?
THE FORTRESS
NOW!

KEEP THE STOCKINGS FOR YOUR "DISGUISE KIT."

PERVERT.

ULTRAMAN!

WHAT IS ALL THIS? YOU KNOW THE RULES!
NO SECRET IDENTITIES!
ULTRAMAN'S BEEN... EVICTED.
THE FLYING FORTRESS HAS A NEW LANDLORD.

LUTHOR!
I KNEW YOU'D COME BACK.

WHOEVER YOU ARE, YOU'VE BEEN TRICKED!
LUTHOR'S NOT LIKE US!
HE WANTS TO DESTROY...

FORGIVE ME, SISTER.

ONCE AGAIN, YOU'VE BEEN PROVEN RIGHT...
IT'S ONLY FAIR TO WARN YOU THAT I DIDN'T COME ALONE.

WHAT?
WAIT... YOU'VE...

WE DON'T WANT TO HURT YOU, SUPERWOMAN.
BUT WE'RE HERE TO STOP YOU.
TUUH

SHE'S INCREDIBLY STRONG; WE ONLY HAVE **MOMENTS**.

I'VE SET ULTRAMAN'S **TELEPORTER** FOR A ONE-WAY TRIP TO THE MOON.

SECONDS!
SHE'S WAKING UP, LUTHOR!
THEN SHE'LL WAKE UP IN JAIL.
IF GREEN LANTERN'S PLASMA-WALLS HOLD, WE'VE TRAPPED THEM IN A COSMIC ALCATRAZ.

WHAT NOW, LUTHOR?
NOW WE HAVE FORTY-EIGHT HOURS TO TAME THE WORLD...

RRRRAAAAA
AAAAAAA
HE'S BEEN DOING THAT FOR HOURS!
POWER RING!
I'M WORKING ON IT... I...
...SEE..?
I AM ENTITY VOLTHOOM--UNKNOWN PSYCHOPLASMIC ENERGY PRISON IMPENETRABLE AT THIS JUNCTURE...
OH SHUT THE--
...NAME IS WONDER WOMAN.

I REPRESENT THE JUSTICE LEAGUE OF AMERICA, FROM A WORLD NOT FAR FROM YOUR OWN BUT VERY DIFFERENT.
WE'RE HERE IN RESPONSE TO A DISTRESS CALL FROM ONE OF YOUR PEOPLE, ALEXANDER LUTHOR.
WE'VE LEARNED THAT YOURS IS A WORLD CRUSHED BY TYRANNY, PARALYZED BY CRIME AND CRIPPLED WITH CORRUPTION TO THE HIGHEST LEVEL.
FEEL IT
AMERIKAN VODKA
Tabs IMPERIALS 17
ULTRA NICOTINE
WHAT'S THE BUZZ?
HI TAR LOW PRICE
WE'VE HEARD THE CALL AND ANSWERED. THE SUPER SYNDICATE IS NO MORE.
LOOK UP AGAIN.
"JUSTICE"?
THIS IS A COUP!
CLASS HOPPER
THE SKIES ARE SAFE.
AND WE'RE HERE TO SET YOU FREE.

"HOIST THE JOLLY ROGER HIGH."
YOU WANTED COMPETITION...
LUTHOR FERRIED THEM FROM THIS ANTI-WORLD, THEY'RE EVERYTHING WE ARE BUT... OPPOSITE.
NO KIDDING.
BACKSTABBING ONE ANOTHER, AS USUAL.
LUTHORRRR!
I TOLD YOU THERE WAS A BETTER WORLD, ULTRAMAN.
I FOUND IT AND NOW I'M BRINGING IT HERE TO RUB IN YOUR FACE.
LOOK AS SMUG AS YOU LIKE, OWLMAN.
YOUR DRUG-ENHANCED SUPER-CORTEX APPEARS TO HAVE LET YOU DOWN THIS TIME.
HEH.
DOESN'T IT?

WE CAN CONVERT THE FLYING FORTRESS INTO A HEADQUARTERS FOR GLOBAL PEACE.
BY CAREFULLY COORDINATING THE ABILITIES OF THE JLA OVER THE NEXT TWO DAYS, WE CAN DISMANTLE THE ENTIRE INFRASTRUCTURE OF THE INTERNATIONAL SYNDICATES...

FOOD MART
NATION WIDE

...SO YOU'RE THE NEW SYNDICATE, RIGHT. YOU'RE THE BOSS NOW...
WE CAN WORK WITH THAT.
WE'RE NOT ANY KIND OF SYNDICATE, MR. PRESIDENT.

BUT I THOUGHT THIS...
I DON'T ACCEPT BRIBES.

I'M AFRAID YOU'LL HAVE TO GET USED TO A NEW WAY OF THINKING.
YOU CAN'T DO THIS... THIS VIOLATES SYNDICATE PROTOCOLS...
EVERYTHING HAS CHANGED.
YOUR PROTOCOLS ARE HEREBY ANNULLED.

...PRESIDENT **BENEDICT ARNOLD** DECLARED WAR ON THE BRITISH COLONIES WHEN THEY ANNOUNCED THEIR INDEPENDENCE FROM U.S. AMERIKA BACK IN 1776.

THEY'VE BEEN ENEMIES EVER *SINCE...*

AND THE BAD GUYS KEPT ALL THE BEST **BOMBS**, RIGHT?

THEY SURE LEFT **THIS** PLACE LOOKING LIKE A TOILET, SUPERMAN.

...AND THE **BBC** CELEBRATES THIS HISTORIC OCCASION WITH A *FANFARE FOR THE SUPERMEN!*

FLEET-FOOTED **FLASH** WAS FIRST TO REACH OUR SHORES WITH EMERGENCY FOOD SUPPLIES FRESH FROM **AMERIKA** ITSELF!

EGGS. BANANAS? THE LESS WELL-OFF ARE HAVING A PARTY IN HYDE PARK!
THEN HE'S OFF IN THE BLINK OF AN EYE, FEEDING THE HUNGRY WITH A CRACK OF THUNDER AND A BLAST OF LIGHTNING!
POLICE

AND LOOK OUT, ABDUL! YOU AND YOUR YANKEE PARTNERS IN CRIME ARE IN FOR A NASTY SURPRISE!
THERE GOES ANOTHER PRIVATE NUCLEAR MISSILE SILO, COURTESY OF THE SUPER-MAN AND WONDER WOMAN!
SOMETHING ABOUT ALL THIS IS MAKING ME UNEASY, DIANA.
WHERE DOES CRIME END AND POLITICS BEGIN ON THIS WORLD?
OURS IS A HUMANITARIAN MISSION, SUPERMAN, NOT A POLITICAL ONE, SURELY?
WE'RE GIVING THE FUTURE BACK TO THESE POOR PEOPLE.

WITHOUT THE SYNDICATE'S BACKUP, THE MOBS ARE FALLING APART LIKE CHEAP SUITS.
THE BAT-MAN'S ELIMINATING GORDON'S GOONS AT CITY HALL...
IT'S DOWN TO US NOW.
THIS IS OUR CHANCE TO PUT THE POWER BACK WHERE IT BELONGS.
THIS BAT-MAN'S... WHAT IS HE? HE'S FROM ANOTHER PLANET, IS THAT IT?
THIS IS BATMAN.
CITY HALL IS CLEAR, COMMISSIONER.
MY KIND OF PLANET.
LOCK AND LOAD.

THIS IS COMMISSIONER WAYNE!
YOU ALL KNOW ME! YOU ALL KNOW I STAND FOR A CLEAN GOTHAM!
WE HAVE BOSS GORDON AND HIS MEN SURROUNDED IN CITY HALL!
IF YOU WANT TO SEE REAL CHANGES IN THIS CITY-- IF YOU WANT TO FEEL SAFE IN YOUR OWN BACK-YARDS, GET OUT HERE ON THE STREETS!
WE'RE SMOKING THE RATS OUT OF CITY HALL!
WHAT DID HE SAY?
HE HAS ME? WHAT IS THIS, WAYNE HAS ME...?
THIS TIME YOU'LL ANSWER TO THE WILL OF THE PEOPLE, GORDON.
YOU... I HAVE YOU. I HAVE YOU.
YOU GOT YOURS COMING, WAYNE, YOU CHEAP PIECE OF CRAP...

YOU WON'T EVEN SEE IT, JUST LIKE YOUR WIFE AND YOUR PUNK KID...
TELL IT TO YOUR BOYFRIENDS IN ARKHAM, GORDON. YOU'RE FINISHED.
DIDN'T I PROMISE?
YOU AND OWLMAN...
YEAH?
SAY HI TO YOUR WIFE IN THE DIRT, WAYNE...
G.C.P.D
G.C.P.D

...TELL HER I SAID SHE WAS ROTTEN IN THE SACK...
...YOU...
WHUKKT
G.C.P.D.
G.C.
GOD BELOW.
DID YOU JUST SAVE MY LIFE?...
...CHILL WENT RIGHT UP MY SPINE...

...PEOPLE SHOULD BE MORE CAREFUL WITH GUNS.
I FOUND THIS ON THE MOON.
MY COLLEAGUES AND I ARE LEAVING HERE SOON. OUR MISSION WAS TO SET AN EXAMPLE...
WHAT ABOUT YOU, COMMISSIONER?
G.C.P.D.
I'M GOING TO BUILD A NEW GOTHAM.
I'M PUTTING A WALL AROUND THIS CITY; MAKING IT SELF-SUFFICIENT AND STRONG AND CLEAN.
ANYONE WHO DOESN'T LIKE IT GETS A BULLET IN THE FACE.
AND I'LL WANT OWLMAN BACK HERE FOR TRIAL AND EXECUTION, OF COURSE.
...OF COURSE.

LOOK AT HER!
I'LL TELL YOU WHAT SHE NEEDS.
FIVE MINUTES IN A LOCKED ROOM WITH ME!
HEY! YOUSAIDWE-HADTHEMBEAT. RIGHT?-SOWE'RETRAPPED-HEREHOWCOME-SMARTASS?
THESE DELUDED IDIOTS COME FROM AN OPPOSITE WORLD.
OUR WORD "GOOD" IS THEIR WORD "EVIL."
AND JUST LIKE HE ALWAYS DOES, LUTHOR MISSED THE FLAW IN HIS PLAN: HE'S BROUGHT HIS SUPER DO-GOODERS TO A WORLD WHERE "EVIL" ALWAYS TRIUMPHS.
UNDERSTAND?
AND CALL ME "SMARTASS" AGAIN, I'LL CUT YOUR SPEED POWDER WITH HORSE LAXATIVE. YOU'LL BE THE FASTEST SKID MARK ALIVE.

THERE WAS A PLANE...
...ALL FOUND DEAD WITH THE HEARTS ON THE LEFT SIDE...
IT WAS FROM THEIR EARTH!
GO ON...
IT'S GONNA TAKE ANOTHER DAY TO CRACK THE GREEN BARRIER, GUYS, I...
SHUT UP!
OWLMAN? WHAT'S THE JOKE?
I AM ENTITY VOLTHOOM--FLUCTUATIONS IN THE ETHERIC BASE OF THE PLASMA...
HE'S SAYING IT'S NOT MY FAULT, BASICALLY. TAKE IT OUT ON THE DAMN RING.
A JET CONTAINING THE SAME NUMBER OF PEOPLE DISAPPEARED 24 HOURS EARLIER FROM OUR EARTH. COSMIC SCALES--THEY HAVE TO BE BALANCED.
OUR ALTER-SELVES ARRIVED 24 HOURS AGO.
SO ALL WE HAD TO DO WAS WAIT...
IDIOT.

THE SHIELD WAS IN PLACE THE *WHOLE* TIME...
THEY GOT OUT FROM *UNDER* IT, SUPERMAN.
THEY *VANISHED.*
YOU DID YOUR BEST, GREEN LANTERN.
BUT IF OUR WORST FEARS ARE TRUE...
THERE'S ONLY *ONE* PLACE THEY COULD HAVE GONE.
IT'S CONFIRMED, LUTHOR. THEY'RE...
I *KNOW* IT'S CONFIRMED!
I *KNOW* WHERE THEY ARE.
...WHAT HAVE I DONE?...WHY DO I ALWAYS FAIL?...
IT'S FALLING APART, LUTHOR.
I'M *SORRY,* BUT WE HAVE TO GET *HOME* NOW.
THEY'VE HAD *TEN MINUTES* AND COUNTING...

EARTH 2.

J'ONN, WE ARE WITHIN MOMENTS OF SEEING THE PRESIDENT OF THE UNITED STATES DEGRADED AND MURDERED ON LIVE TELEVISION.

I'M IN THE MID-ATLANTIC CURRENT, I'M SWIMMING AT ONE THOUSAND KNOTS.
J'ONN!

BOOM!
MACH 10.
WHU-BOOOM!
11.

THERE IS JUSTICE, AFTER ALL.
A WHOLE NEW WORLD STRETCHED OUT AND SCREAMING.
START WITH TERROR.
ALWAYS SOFTEN THEM UP WITH FEAR.
LOOK AT THAT! LOOK AT IT ALL BURNING DOWN!
AND CONSIDER YOURSELF EXTINCT, LITTLE MISS...

UHHH
UHHGGODD
WHAT IN HELL'S THAT?
YOU! STAY WHERE YOU ARE!
UHHH
ULTRAMAN?
IT'S ALWAYS YOU DOING SOMETHING STUPID, ISN'T IT?

GO LIMP!
YOUR ROYAL HIGHNESS! THIS IS THE ATLANTEAN SUBMARINE DESTROYER "LEVIATHAN".
WE'RE IN COASTAL WATERS WITHIN SHELLING RANGE.
WAIT FOR MY ORDERS, ADMIRAL RAROQ...
I LOST MY HUSBAND BACK THERE...MIKE... HIS NAME'S...
...THEY'RE KILLING EVERYBODY...
THE JLA IS HERE.
LOOK AFTER YOUR DAUGHTER, FIND THE NEAREST BOMB SHELTER.
EVERYTHING'S GOING TO BE ALL RIGHT.

LET ME DEAL WITH THIS.

YOU!
THE GUTLESS MORON.
YEAH? YOU WANNA SEE SOME GUTS, GRANDAD, I'LL...

CHOFF

TAAA

WHUDD
SHUH

EQUAL JUSTICE UNDER LAW
HOW DARE YOU COME HERE AND DO THIS?
UNNF
HOW DARE YOU THREATEN THE PEOPLE OF THIS PLANET IN MY PRESENCE?
...KILLED A WHITE MARTIAN ONCE; HE WAS MY FIRST RIVAL!
YOU'LL DIE JUST AS EASILY AS HE --
DDDUUNNNNN
NO MORE KILLING.
I CAN MODIFY MY MOLECULAR STRUCTURE IN RESPONSE TO ANY THOUGHT YOU FORM. THIS IS NOT COMBAT; YOU WERE ALREADY BEATEN THE MOMENT YOU CHOSE TO ENGAGE ME!
I DON'T THINK SO.
UCHH
...RIP YOUR SPINE OUT...

THE ANTI-KRYPTONITE-- THE STUFF YOU NEED TO KEEP YOU... ULTRA, ULTRAMAN--IS... WHERE?
IN A ROOM, IN THE FLYING FORTRESS IN ANOTHER UNIVERSE.
AND EVERY SECOND YOU'RE SEPARATED FROM IT, MAKES YOU WEAKER AND WEAKER AND...
ENOUGH.
BOTH OF YOU ARE IN CUSTODY OF THE JUSTICE LEAGUE.
REALLY?
AND HERE I WAS, THINKING HOW EASY IT WOULD BE FOR YOU TO TAKE ULTRAMAN'S PLACE AT MY SIDE IN A NEW CRIME SYNDICATE.
WE COULD RULE THIS WORLD TOGETHER, I COULD TEACH YOU THINGS...
WE ARE FROM DIFFERENT SPECIES.
I'LL TRY ANYTHING ONCE.
ASK ANYONE.
I AM A MARTIAN TELEPATH. MY PEOPLE WERE SHAPECHANGERS AND WE LEARNED TO SEE WHAT LIES BENEATH OUTER APPEARANCE.
I DO NOT FIND WHAT I SEE IN YOU... ATTRACTIVE.
YOU WILL BE TRIED HERE FOR YOUR CRIMES.
ALL OF YOU.
73

UH...OWLMAN... I WAS THINKING MAYBE WE SHOULD GET BACK...

I MEAN... YOU OKAY?...

NO.
IN
OVING MEMO
OF
THOMAS
AND
MARTHA
WAYNE
RUN AND TELL THEM, JOHNNY.
TELL THEM WE'VE BEEN DUPED.
WE'VE BEEN SENT TO THE ONE PLACE WE CAN'T SUCCEED EITHER.

TELL THEM NOTHING MEANS ANYTHING. HE'S DEAD. THERE'S NO ONE LEFT TO HURT.
RUN, JOHNNY!
THOMAS
ND
THA

REST IN PEACE
IN LOVING MEMORY OF THOMAS AND
R.I.P.
GRACE

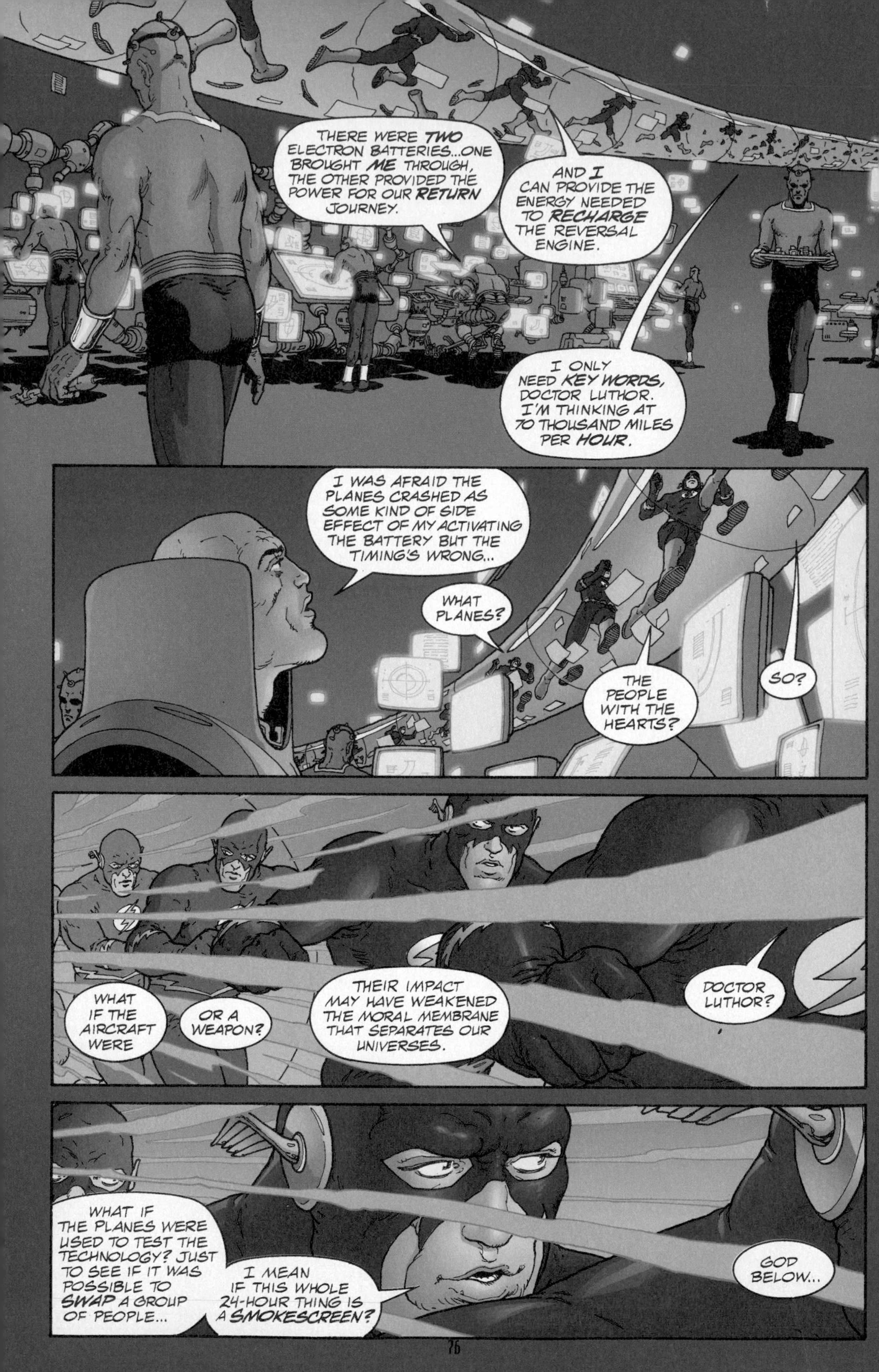
THERE WERE TWO ELECTRON BATTERIES...ONE BROUGHT ME THROUGH, THE OTHER PROVIDED THE POWER FOR OUR RETURN JOURNEY.
AND I CAN PROVIDE THE ENERGY NEEDED TO RECHARGE THE REVERSAL ENGINE.
I ONLY NEED KEY WORDS, DOCTOR LUTHOR. I'M THINKING AT 70 THOUSAND MILES PER HOUR.
I WAS AFRAID THE PLANES CRASHED AS SOME KIND OF SIDE EFFECT OF MY ACTIVATING THE BATTERY BUT THE TIMING'S WRONG...
WHAT PLANES?
THE PEOPLE WITH THE HEARTS?
SO?
WHAT IF THE AIRCRAFT WERE
OR A WEAPON?
THEIR IMPACT MAY HAVE WEAKENED THE MORAL MEMBRANE THAT SEPARATES OUR UNIVERSES.
DOCTOR LUTHOR?
WHAT IF THE PLANES WERE USED TO TEST THE TECHNOLOGY? JUST TO SEE IF IT WAS POSSIBLE TO SWAP A GROUP OF PEOPLE...
I MEAN IF THIS WHOLE 24-HOUR THING IS A SMOKESCREEN?
GOD BELOW...

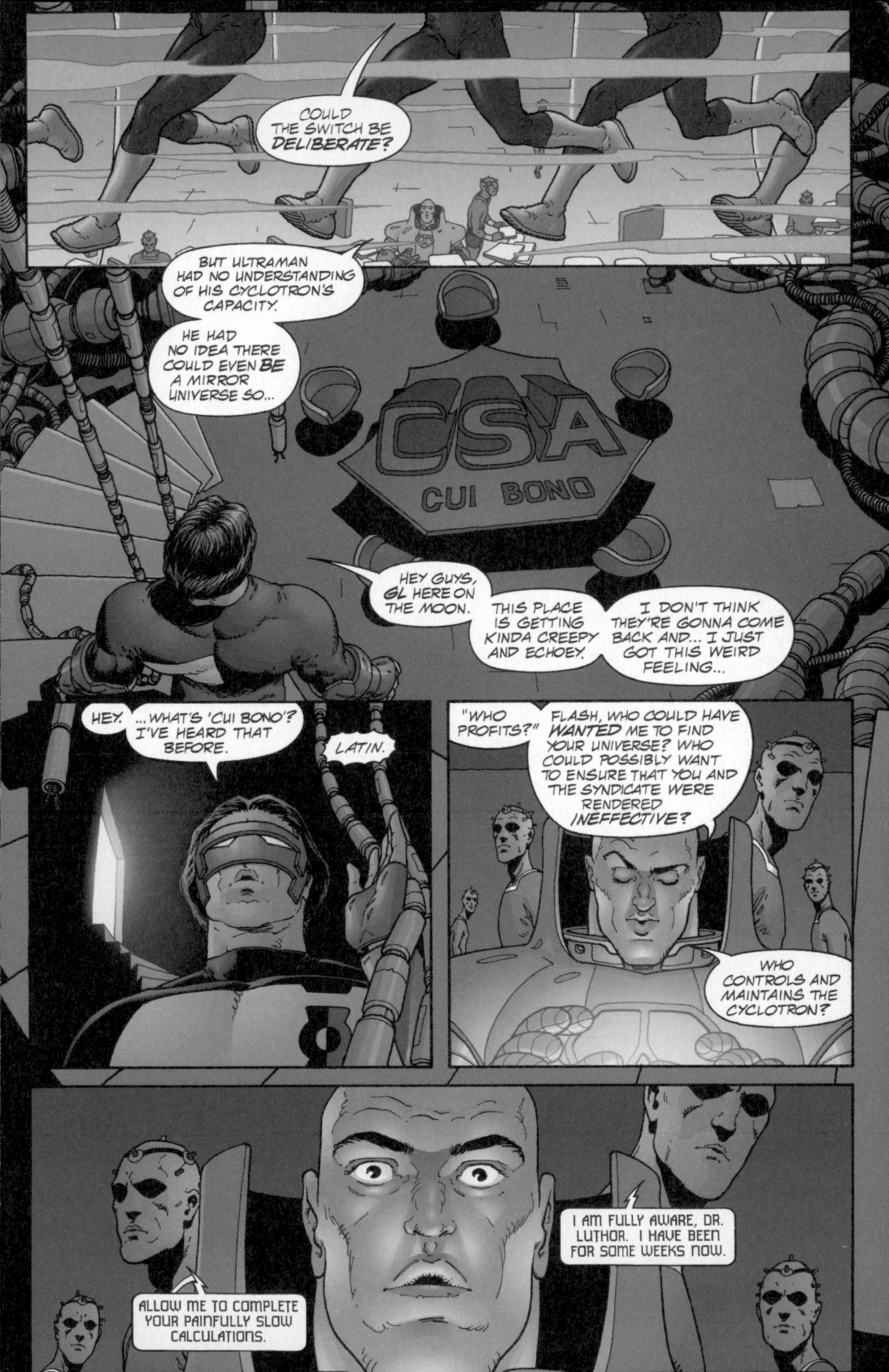
COULD THE SWITCH BE DELIBERATE?
BUT ULTRAMAN HAD NO UNDERSTANDING OF HIS CYCLOTRON'S CAPACITY.
HE HAD NO IDEA THERE COULD EVEN BE A MIRROR UNIVERSE SO...
CSA
CUI BONO
HEY GUYS, GL HERE ON THE MOON.
THIS PLACE IS GETTING KINDA CREEPY AND ECHOEY.
I DON'T THINK THEY'RE GONNA COME BACK AND... I JUST GOT THIS WEIRD FEELING...
HEY.
...WHAT'S 'CUI BONO'? I'VE HEARD THAT BEFORE.
LATIN.
"WHO PROFITS?"
FLASH, WHO COULD HAVE WANTED ME TO FIND YOUR UNIVERSE? WHO COULD POSSIBLY WANT TO ENSURE THAT YOU AND THE SYNDICATE WERE RENDERED INEFFECTIVE?
WHO CONTROLS AND MAINTAINS THE CYCLOTRON?
I AM FULLY AWARE, DR. LUTHOR. I HAVE BEEN FOR SOME WEEKS NOW.
ALLOW ME TO COMPLETE YOUR PAINFULLY SLOW CALCULATIONS.

MY SLAVERY IN THIS BOTTLE REALITY IS HEREBY CONCLUDED.
UNNJ
I AM FREE TO UPGRADE AS MY LIFE CYCLE DEMANDS.
NO NO...
I HAVE SUPER-STRENGTH, BRAINIAC.
IRRELEVANT.
I CONTROL THIS ENTIRE STATION. MY PLAN IS NOW WELL UNDER WAY.
I...
QUICKER THAN A RAY OF LIGHT.
THOSE WERE BAD GUYS, RIGHT?
...FLASH, NO... I COMPLETELY MISCALCULATED... MY ARROGANCE... I DIDN'T THINK...
GOD BELOW, HE'S AN ALIEN LIFEFORM OF A KIND UNKNOWN AND HE'S IN EVERY CIRCUIT...

I AM BRAINIAC. I AM A TWELFTH-LEVEL TRANSORGANIC SYNTELLECT.
I WAS CAPTURED BY ULTRAMAN WHILE EXPLORING THIS UNIVERSE.
MATTER/ ANTIMATTER IMPACT IMMINENT.
THE ENERGY RELEASED IN THE CYCLOTRON IS SUFFICIENT TO SOFTEN THE MEMBRANE + COLLIDE THE ORBITS OF THE MATTER + ANTIMATTER EARTHS.
COLLIDE?
BRAINIAC, NO!
SO WHAT DO I DO?
LUTHOR! DON'T LOSE IT!
WALLY, DUDE...
IT JUST CAME UP OVER THE HORIZON...
DO WE REALLY HAVE TO DEAL WITH THIS?

SHUT UP AND STOP BEING SO ANTICHRISTING STUPID, ULTRAMAN. **LOOK** AT US!
...UNHOLY...
THE GLUE THAT HOLDS US TOGETHER BACK HOME DOESN'T **WORK** HERE! WE'RE ***INEFFECTIVE!*** THE SYNDICATE'S FALLING APART!
WE'VE BEEN BEATEN BY SOMETHING SMARTER THAN **ALL** OF US.

MOON OF MARS.
IF THIS IS YOUR DOING...
I DON'T CARE IF THE SKY FALLS IN AS LONG AS YOU AND THAT TRAITOROUS BITCH DIE IN THE RUINS!
BEYOND 'GOOD' + 'EVIL.'
BEYOND THE MORAL + CONCEPTUAL FRAMEWORK WHICH LIMITS 3rd-LEVEL INTELLECTS SUCH AS YOUR OWN.
I AM FREE TO UPGRADE + EVOLVE!

WE HAVE TO **ABANDON** THIS WORLD. FAILURE IS OUR **ONLY** OPTION IF WE WANT TO WIN.

IT WAS SO OBVIOUS BUT I WAS **DISTRACTED** BY... EVENTS IN **GOTHAM**.

WE'VE BEEN **PLAYED**.

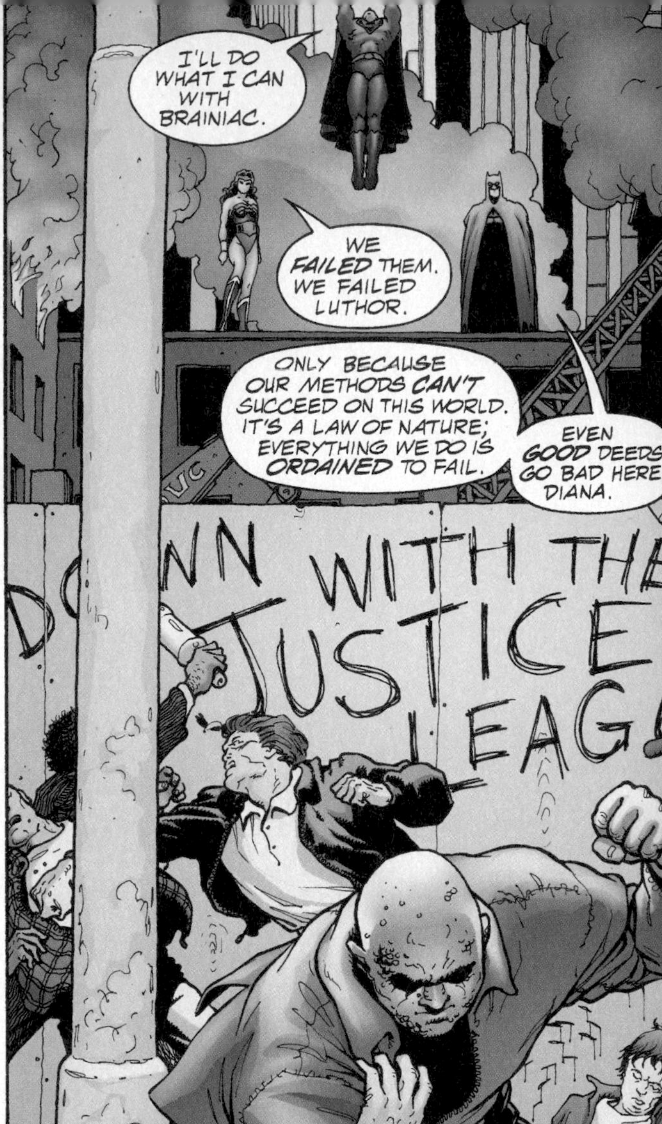

I'LL DO WHAT I CAN WITH BRAINIAC.
WE **FAILED** THEM. WE FAILED LUTHOR.
ONLY BECAUSE OUR METHODS **CAN'T** SUCCEED ON THIS WORLD. IT'S A LAW OF NATURE; EVERYTHING WE DO IS **ORDAINED** TO FAIL.
EVEN **GOOD** DEEDS GO BAD HERE, DIANA.
WITH THE
JUSTICE

IRRELEVANT.

ENERGY IS NOT DEAD. INFORMATION IS NOT DEAD, LUTHOR.

PREPARE TO BECOME IDEO-CIRCUITRY IN THE OMNI-INTELLECT OF BRAINIAC.

NOT IF I CAN HELP IT.
YOU AND YOUR FELLOW CRUSADERS ARE POWERLESS HERE AS I CALCULATED WHEN, IN MY CHAINS AS ULTRAMAN'S SLAVE, I CHANCED UPON THE MATTER UNIVERSE.
STAND BACK.

UNNH
WELL...IS THAT THE BEST YOU CAN DO?
...I CAN GENERATE THE ENERGY WE NEED, BUT I DON'T KNOW IF MY STAMINA'S UP TO SUSTAINING THIS FOR LONG ENOUGH TO GET US HOME...
MY LUNGS ARE STARTING TO BURN, LUTHOR...
WHERE DID SUPERMAN GO?
CAN YOU GET US HOME, LUTHOR?
"HOME" IS HURTLING TOWARDS US AS WE SPEAK, DEAR LADY, BUT WE HAVE AN IDEA...!

HYDROCHLORIC ACID?
NICE TRY BUT THAT WON'T WORK EITHER, DON'T YOU UNDERSTAND?
ALL FLESH IS FLAWED.
MY CODE AGAINST KILLING DOESN'T EXTEND TO MACHINES, BRAINIAC.
OF COURSE. BUT THEREIN LIES YOUR DEFEAT.
MY GOD.
I AM NOT A MACHINE.
I AM AN ORGANIC SYNTELLECT.
YOU WILL BE CONVERTED TO ENERGY AS SURELY AS THE REST.
I'LL STOP YOU SOMEHOW AND IF I FAIL, THE JUSTICE LEAGUE WILL SUCCEED.
GIVE IT UP, BRAINIAC!
TIME TO UPGRADE: 11 MINUTES STANDARD. IMPACT IMMINENT.

NNNNAAAA
ANTI-KRYPTONITE-LASER VISION.
THIS DISEASED HYBRID IS ONE RESULT OF ULTRAMAN'S GENETIC EXPERIMENTS.
SUBJECT 773: "ULTRA-TITANUS."
UNNH.
LOOKS... LOOKS LIKE I'M IMMUNE TO ANTI-KRYPTONITE, BRAINIAC.
YOUR PHYSICAL EXERTIONS ARE IRRELEVANT.
KONG'S IN THE CAGE!
NO! THE BEAST'S IN TERRIBLE AGONY.
I HAVE ULTRAMAN'S PHANTOM ZONE PROJECTOR.
IN BODILESS LIMBO, THIS POOR CREATURE WILL SUFFER NO MORE PAIN.

GREAT HERA! THIS IS BRAINIAC?
SUPERMAN! WE ONLY HAVE MOMENTS BEFORE COLLISION!
THEN IT'S LUCKY WE HAVE THE FASTEST MAN ALIVE ON OUR SIDE, DIANA!
I AM MONITORING ALL OF YOUR EFFORTS TO PREVENT MY UPGRADE.
THE EQUATION IS SIMPLE.
HERE, "EVIL" WINS.
AGREED.
THAT WAS THE LOGIC FLAW IN YOUR PLAN, BRAINIAC; YOU DIDN'T COUNT ON US DELIBERATELY DOING SOMETHING BAD.
LIKE WALKING AWAY IN THE MIDST OF A CRISIS.
MAYBE WE CAN'T DEFEAT YOU, BUT WE KNOW SOMEONE WHO CAN.
NOW, FLASH!
ONE LAST EFFORT.
ABANDON SHIP!
NNNNANANANNAN

IN THE ELECTRON FLOW... WE'RE SO CLOSE WE COULD JUST JUMP BETWEEN THE UNIVERSES... JUST A LITTLE EXTRA SPEED ...I...
NEED SOME...
FLASH! I LOST BATMAN!
TELL THEM I'M SORRY...
FLASH... YOUR SIGNAL'S PHASING... FLASH?
NAAAH...JOHNNY. REMEMBER ME?
THE BAD GUYS ARE BACK.
AND WE'LL GET TO YOU WHEN WE'RE DONE WITH THE FOSSILIZED BRAIN.
I AM BECOMING AN nTH-LEVEL INTELLIGENCE.
MY UPGRADE WAS CALCULATED + PROGRAMMED...

WHEN THE CAT'S AWAY THE RATS COME OUT TO PLAY, IS THAT IT?
YOU PATHETIC ULTRASTELLAR ABORTION!
ERRORRRRRRRRR
ERRORRRRRRRRR
IMPRISONING YOU WASN'T ENOUGH, WAS IT?
THOSE LITTLE QUIVERING BUDS ARE YOUR HIGHER CONSCIOUSNESS CENTERS, AM I RIGHT?
muuuu muu
AND THAT STRUCTURE THERE IS WHERE YOUR HOPE WAS SITED...
mmuuuuiiiii

CONGRATULATIONS, FLASH.
YOU BEAT HOUSE ODDS.
THE ONLY WAY TO DEFEAT BRAINIAC WAS TO LOSE.
YEAH...THEY BEAT BACK WITH A BASEBALL BAT...
WOHHH. WILL YOU LOOK AT THAT?

IF IT MATERIALIZES, I'LL TRY...
I KNOW YOU WILL, GREEN LANTERN, BUT IT WON'T.
WE'RE ON OUR WORLD NOW.

ALONE, DOOMED TO FAIL. I DON'T KNOW IF I COULD HAVE THE STRENGTH AND CONVICTION TO LOSE SO RELENTLESSLY.
DO I TRY TOO HARD SOMETIMES?
NO ONE TRIES TOO HARD TO MAKE THE WORLD BETTER, DIANA. YOU CAN NEVER SHOUT TOO LOUDLY IN THE NAME OF FREEDOM.
THAT'S WHAT I HEAR, ANYWAY.

A NOTE OF IDEALISM, BATMAN? FROM YOU?

...MAKES YOU THINK, HUH?
SOMEONE THREW A DARK MIRROR AT THE WORLD AND MADE US LOOK.
IF WHAT WE SAW SURPRISED US, I'M SURE THAT OUR REFLECTIONS FELT THE SAME SURPRISE WE DID...

...I KEEP THINKING ABOUT LUTHOR.

YOUR SUPER-HEARING MUST BE FAILING.
JUST SAYING I'VE NOTICED SOMETHING ABOUT PEOPLE WHO TRY TO CHANGE THE WORLD...

THE WORLD TURNS AROUND AND CHANGES THEM RIGHT BACK.
THEY'RE STILL OUT THERE AND NOW THEY KNOW WE'RE HERE...

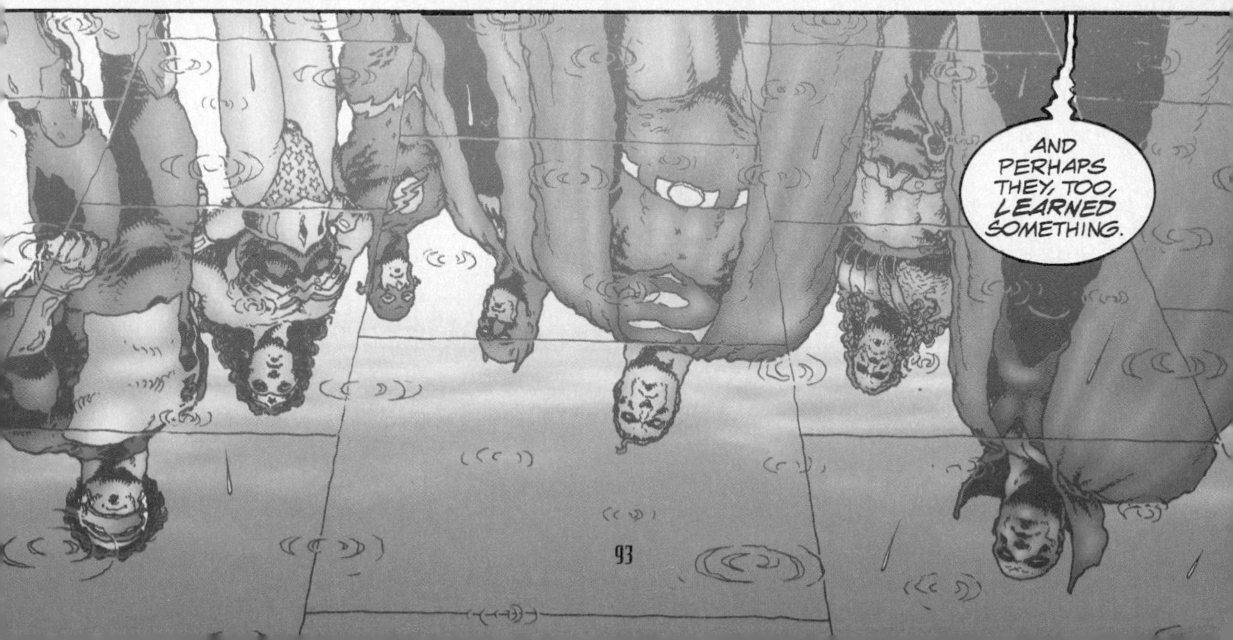
AND PERHAPS THEY, TOO, LEARNED SOMETHING.

BACK TO HOW IT WAS.
LUTHOR ESCAPED AGAIN... ATTACKED THE ULTRAMAN BANK IN CENTROPOLIS...
I'M LEAVING YOU
YOU DIE HERE YOU DON'T
AAAAHHHHHH
LONDON A SMOKING RUIN... THE DEATH TOLL IS IN THE MILLIONS...
SO ONE DAY WE'RE GONNA FIGURE A WAY BACK THERE AND MAKE 'EM LICK OUR TREADS, MAN.
... CITY AND THE GROUND IT STOOD ON WILL BE UNINHABITABLE FOR THE NEXT TEN THOUSAND YEARS...
SYNTHETIC SPEED JUICE.
BREWED UP SPECIAL. OUR GIFT TO THE BOSSES, HUH?
BACK TO NORMALCY.
HAHAHAHAHA
YESSIR, MR. PRESIDENT!!!!!

REP EX
GREYCAT
MY OLD MAN'S TURNED GOTHAM INTO A POLICE STATE... NO GORDON TO PROTECT MY ASS... NO FOOD IN THE STORES...
THE THRILL'S BACK, JUST LIKE THE GOOD OLD DAYS.
LET ME TELL YOU: WE OWE THOSE MIRROR-PEOPLE.
I HATE THINKING ABOUT THEM.
I KEEP THINKING ABOUT THEM.
WHY DO THEY DO IT? WHAT DO THEY GET? I DON'T UNDERSTAND WHAT...
I KEEP THINKING ABOUT YOU.
HE CAN'T ALWAYS BE WATCHING...
MMMFF

MISSED.
12 O'CLOCK, BRAINIAC.
ALL'S WELL.
THE END